AWESOME JOKES 5 EVERY YEAR OLD SHOULD KNOW!

chancesFOR CHiLDREN
BUTTLEuk

All profits from this book go to children's charities. To find out more, visit matwaugh.co.uk/charity

PROUDLY SUPPORTING
ellenor. x
for families facing terminal illness

Additional research: Olivera Ristovska

Design: Fanni Williams / thehappycolourstudio.com
Icons: Freepik, Smashicons, Kiranshastry, Creattica, Icon Pond, Dinosoft Lab &
mynamepong from www.flaticon.com

www.matwaugh.co.uk

Produced by Big Red Button Books,
a division of Say So Media Ltd.

ISBN: 978-1-9999147-1-4

Published: May 2018
This edition: July 2019

AWESOME JOKES

5 EVERY YEAR OLD SHOULD KNOW!

MAT WAUGH

ILLUSTRATIONS BY YURKO RYMAR

Introduction

What is funny?

Is it when your brother gets stuck in the mud? I think that's quite funny.

Is it when milk spurts out of your nose? I think that's very funny.

Or is it anything that gives you a happy feeling? Stuff that makes you laugh so hard that your tummy hurts and your eyes do a little wee?

I hope you find jokes like that in this book. They're my very best jokes for 5 year olds.

Let's Get Cracking!

What wobbles as it flies?
A jellycopter!

What's black and white, black and white, black and white?
Penguins rolling down a hill!

Why are carrots good for your eyes?
Because otherwise all the rabbits would
need glasses!

**What kind of button is
impossible to undo?**
Your belly button!

What do you give a sick bird?
Tweet-ment!

What do little trees say on Halloween?
Twig or treat!

What is a centipede's favourite toy?

Leg-o!

What do you call Santa Claus on a break?
Santa Pause!

What do policemen have in their sandwiches?
Traffic jam!

 **What do cows do on Valentine's Day?**
Smooooooch! *(bleurgh!)*

If mummies are from Egypt, where are daddies from?
(Perhaps the Planet Zog? And why isn't it Daddy's turn to make the dinner today?)

Why can't you give a girl called Elsa a balloon?

Because she will *Let it Go!*

Knock Knock! — **Who's there?**
Noah.
Noah who?
Noah body wants to play with me! Will you?

TONGUE TWISTER

Red leather yellow leather
Try saying this really fast ten times – it's really hard!

Why do sheep enjoy going to the movies?
Because they love the snaaaacks!

What do you call a bear with no teeth?
A gummy bear!

Which snack always makes you jump?
POP-corn!

What is a ghost's favourite snack?

Boo-berries!

What do black cats always take to the beach?
A sand-witch!

What do you get if you sit under a cow?

A pat on the head!

What did the dog say when he unwrapped his bone?

That's the pawfect present!

Where do sick wasps go?

To waspital!

Have you heard the joke about the rope?
Sorry, I've decided to skip it.

What does Pooh walk on?
His bear feet!

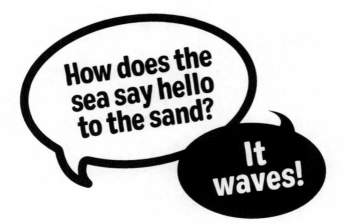

How does the sea say hello to the sand?

It waves!

 **Who's there?**
Justin.
Justin who?
Justin time for dinner!

What did the blanket say to the bed?
Don't worry, I've got you covered!

What do snowmen eat for breakfast?
Frosted Flakes!

Which fruit is never lonely?
A pear!

What did the crab say when he came back from his walking holiday?
Long time, no sea!

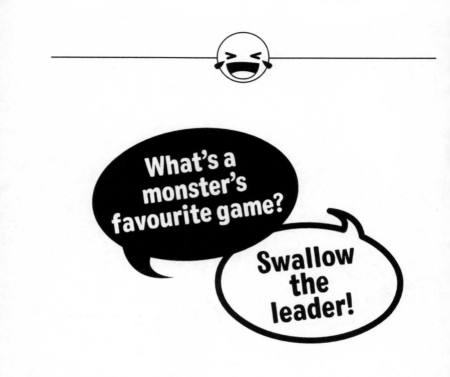

What's a monster's favourite game?

Swallow the leader!

What's a parrot's favourite game?
Hide and beak!

And what's an orange's favourite game?
Duck, duck, juice!

What do you call a boy lying on your doorstep?

Mat.

(This is my Number 1 joke. Can you guess why?)

Here's a tricky one to say quickly! **How can a clam cram in a clean cream can?**

TONGUE TWISTER

Where do apes sleep?
In apri-cots!

Who's the worst card player
in the jungle?
The cheetah!

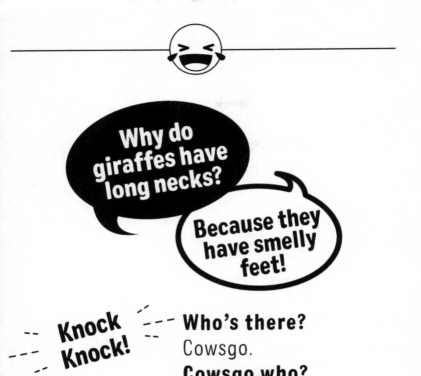

Why do giraffes have long necks?

Because they have smelly feet!

Knock Knock! **Who's there?**
Cowsgo.
Cowsgo who?
No, cows go MOO you silly billy!

Why shouldn't you do sums in the jungle?
Because if you add four and four you get ate!

What's brown, sounds like a bell and comes out of a cow?
DUNG!

What's red and sits on the naughty step?
A shouty tomato!

Who's there?
Tis.
Tis who?
Bless you! How long have you had that cold?

TONGUE TWISTER

This is a tricky one!
I saw a saw that could out saw any other saw I ever saw.

Waiter, Waiter!

What is this fly doing in my soup?
Trying to get out, sir!

Why did the super hero cross the road?
To get to the supermarket of course!

What did the carrot say to the rabbit?
Do you fancy grabbing a bite?

How do you take a snake's temperature?
Very carefully!

Knock Knock! **Who's there?**
Silly.
Silly who?
Silly you,
that's who!

How can I stop sleep walking?
Try sprinkling pieces of Lego on your bedroom floor!

What has four legs but can't walk?
Two pairs of trousers!

Will February March?

No, but April May!

What did the wolf say when he met the little pig?

Very pleased to eat you!

Why did the elephant paint himself lots of different colours?

So he could hide in the crayon box!

Where do sheep get their hair cut?
At the baa-bers!

Knock Knock!

Who's there?
Thea.
Thea who?
Thea later, alligator!

Waiter, Waiter!

There's a fly in the butter!
Yes sir, it's a butterfly.

What did the mother broom say to the baby broom as she tucked him up in bed?
It's time to go to sweep!

What do frogs drink before bed?
Hot croako!

What do you call a bee born in May?
A maybe!

Why can't elephants ride bicycles?
Because they don't have a thumb to ring the bell!

What do you get if you cross a river, a lake and an ocean?
Really wet!

Why is it cold at Christmas?
Because it's in Decembrrrrrrrr!

Knock Knock!

Who's there?
Kanga!
Kanga who?
Nearly right –
it's kangaroo!

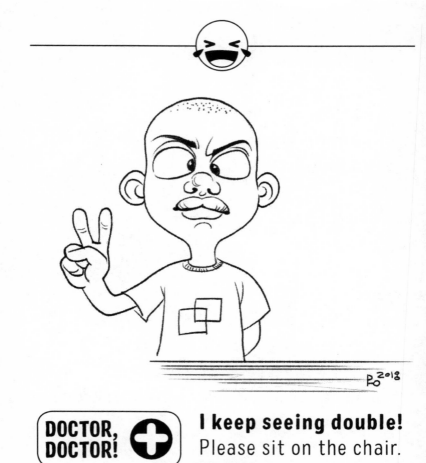

DOCTOR, DOCTOR! ✚ **I keep seeing double!**
Please sit on the chair.
Which one?

Why did the bike stop for a rest?
It was two-tyred!
(You might need a grown-up to explain this!)

Which hand should you use to cut a cake?
You should use a knife instead!

What did the pirate say on her 80th birthday?
Aye matey!
(Clue: say it out loud in a pirate voice!)

Why are snail shells shiny?

Snail varnish!

 **Who's there?**
Beef.
Beef who?
Before I get cold,
let me in!

Can you jump higher than a house?
Of course I can: houses can't jump!

**What do you call a
puppy in the rain?**
A soggy doggy!

What do you call a bee that's never happy?
A grumble bee!

What do monkeys sing at Christmas?
Jungle Bells!

DOCTOR, DOCTOR!

I think I'm turning into a sheep.
How do you feel?
Baaaaaaaad!

TONGUE TWISTER

I scream, you scream, we all scream for ice cream!
Say it 10 times quickly!

Knock Knock!

Who's there?
Water.
Water who?
Water you doing?
Open the door!

What brush should you never use for your hair?
A toilet brush!
(That would be disgusting!)

Why are rivers rich?

They have two banks!

Knock Knock! **Who's there?**
Wooden shoe.
Wooden shoe who?
Wooden shoe like to know?

What does a snowman eat for lunch?
An iceburger!

Waiter, Waiter!

This meal is disgusting! Call the manager!

I'm afraid he won't eat it either, sir.

What fish do millionaires like best?

Gold fish!

How did the crab get to the shops?
Using the sidewalk of course!
(This joke only works in America – do you know the reason why?)

Who's there?
Pasta.
Pasta who?
Pasta key through the letterbox, I'm locked out!

When is the best time of year to go on a trampoline?
Spring time!

Who's there?
Cargo.
Cargo who?
No, cars go BEEP, you silly billy!

What do you call someone who loves cocoa?
A coco-nut!

What do you get if you cross a cow with a grass cutter?
A lawn mooer!

 **Knock Knock!** **Who's there?**
Cockadoodle!
Cockadoodle who?
No, it's cockadoodle doo!
You really *are* a silly billy!

What's small, wobbly and cries a lot?
A jelly baby!

Why was the hungry soccer player sent off?
He couldn't stop dribbling!

What game do horses like?
Stable tennis!

Why did the gnome blush?
Because he did a wee in his flowerbed.

 **Who's there?**
Boo.
Boo who?
Don't get upset, it's just a knock knock joke!

What lives in the ocean and carries 64 people?
An octobus!

What do you call a donkey with 3 legs?
A wonkey!

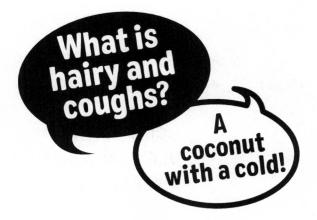

What pillar is no good for building houses?
A caterpillar!

Why did the man with one hand cross the road?
To get to the second-hand shop!

My wife thinks she's a washing line.
You should bring her in, that sounds serious.
But who will hold all my washing?

What falls in winter but never gets hurt?
Snow!

What do you call a crazy duck?
Quackers!

Knock Knock!

Who's there?
Some bunny!
Some bunny who?
Some bunny has been eating all my carrots!

There's a button in my soup!
Oh, thank you, sir. I've been looking for that everywhere!

What do birds give out on Halloween?

Tweets!

Knock Knock!

Who's there?
Smell mop.
Smell mop who?
No, that's disgusting!

TONGUE TWISTER

Get those lips ready!
Shellfish selfish.
Selfish shellfish.
Shellfish selfish.
It's not easy, is it?

Knock Knock!

Who's there?
You!
You who?
Yoo-hoo to you too!

Why didn't the crab share his toys?
He was feeling shellfish!

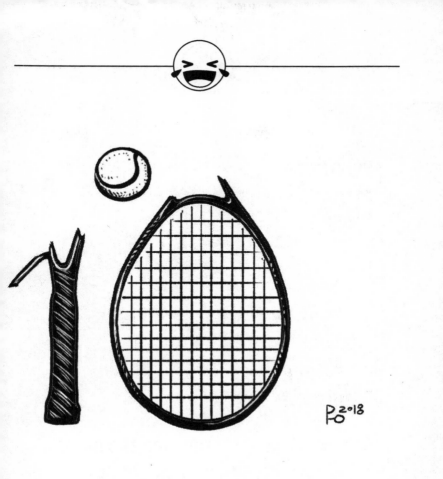

Knock Knock!

Who's there?
Tennis.
Tennis who?
Tennis my favourite number!

What do you call a hippo with chicken pox?
A hippo-spot-amus!

What's the difference between an elephant and peanut butter?
An elephant doesn't stick to the roof of your mouth!

Why can't your nose be 12 inches long?
Because then it would be a foot!

DOCTOR, DOCTOR!

I keep thinking I'm a caterpillar!
Don't worry, you'll soon see a big change.

What do you call a belt that knows when you should have lunch?
A waist of time!

What position does a ghost like to play in soccer?
Ghoulie!

What's an elephant's favourite vegetable?
Squash!

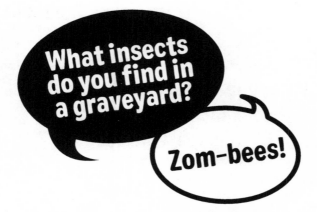

What insects do you find in a graveyard?

Zom-bees!

Knock Knock!

Who's there?
Interrupting pirate.
Interrup...
ARRRRRR!

DOCTOR, DOCTOR!

I feel like a pig!
How long have you been feeling like this?
Oh, about a weeeeeeeeeeeeek!

Where do you learn to make ice cream?
Sundae school!

What happened to the silly man who slept with his head under the pillow?
When he woke up he found that the fairies had taken all his teeth out!

Why did the tomato get left behind?
Because he couldn't ketchup!

Want to make someone look silly?
Just ask them this!
Is there a hole in your shoe?
No? Well how did you get your foot in then?

Why are fish so clever?

They live in schools!

What's purple and 5000 miles long?
The Grape Wall of China!

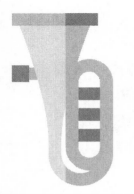

What musical instrument can you find in the bathroom?
A tuba toothpaste!

Why did the boy run around his bed?
He was trying to catch up on his sleep!

Every time I drink a cup of tea I get a stabbing pain in my eye!
Try taking the spoon out first!

Did you hear about the magic tractor?
It turned into a field!

Knock Knock! **Who's there?**
Stopwatch.
Stopwatch who?
Stopwatch you're doing
and tell me another joke!

What's invisible and smells like carrots?

Rabbit trumps!

Where do you find a dog with no legs?
Wherever you left him!

Now it's your turn!

Here are some awesome jokes sent in by 5-year-olds from around the world. Do you know any funny jokes?

What cheese can you hide a horse in?
Mascarpone!
(From Lucy, Peterborough)

Knock Knock! **Who's there?**
Dismay.
Dismay who?
Dismay may be a joke but it doesn't make me laugh.
(From Summer, Charvil)

Sent in by James, aged 5 from Kent

Why was six afraid of seven?
Because seven eight nine!

How funny was that?

If you or your child enjoyed the jokes in this book, I'm really pleased! (If not, please write your complaint on a fifty pound note and send to my address straight away).

If you're feeling kind, there's something really important you can do for me – rate this book on Amazon.

If you do write something nice, let me know – I promise I'll write back. My email address for jokes, notes and more is jokes@matwaugh.co.uk

If you can read this, you're eating enough carrots.

Mat

I know a great joke!

Send me your best joke and I'll put it on my **World Map of Awesome Jokes**!

Head over to the map now to discover silly jokes, clever jokes and weird jokes. Some jokes rhyme, some are a crime, but they're all sent in by children like you!

Will you be the first on the map from your town?

Put your awesome joke here at
www.matwaugh.co.uk/jokemap

About Mat Waugh

It's funny what makes you laugh, isn't it? Sometimes it's a great joke, and I hope you found a few in this book. Sometimes you don't even need words. It could be a funny look from a friend. Or maybe it's something that wasn't supposed to happen.

Once, when I was about six, I was in the back of my aunt's car on a Christmas Day. The sun reflected brightly in the deep puddles from the night's rain.

My aunt wasn't very good at driving. As we approached a dip in the road we could see a vicar cycling towards us, on his way to church. Dad told my aunt to slow down... but she pressed the wrong pedal. The car hit the water with a mighty SPLOOSH! I looked back to see a huge wave swamping the vicar and his bike. He shook his fists at us, but my aunt didn't even notice. I'm still laughing... but I bet the vicar isn't.

I have three daughters to make me laugh now. (Not all the time though: they drive me bananas.)

I live in Tunbridge Wells, which is a lively, lovely town in the south east of England. It's not a very funny place, mind you....

I've always written a lot. I've done lots of writing for other people – mostly serious stuff – but now I write silly, crazy and funny books as well.

Talking of crazy, I had a mad year when I thought I wanted to be a teacher. But then I found out how hard teachers work and that you have to buy your own biscuits. So now I just visit schools to eat their snacks and talk to children about stories.

Last thing: I love hearing from readers. Thoughts, jokes... anything. If that's you, then get in touch.

✉ mail@matwaugh.co.uk
www.matwaugh.co.uk

Or, if you're old enough:

 facebook.com/matwaughauthor
twitter.com/matwaugh

Three more to try!

Cheeky Charlie vol 1-6
Meet Harriet and her small, stinky brother. Together, they're trouble. Fabulously funny stories for kids aged 6 and up.

Fantastic Wordsearches
Wordsearch with a difference: themed, crossword clues and hidden words await!

What's the Magic Word?
It's Alfie's birthday, but it's not going to plan! If only he could remember the magic word - can you help him? For forgetful children aged 4+.

Available from Amazon and local bookshops.

Be the first to know about new stuff! Sign up for my emails at matwaugh.co.uk

Made in the USA
San Bernardino, CA
01 November 2019